Francis Frith's
# Picturesque
# Harbours

*Photographic Memories*

# Francis Frith's
# Picturesque
# Harbours

Dr. Raymond Solly

First published in the United Kingdom in 2002 by
Frith Book Company Ltd

Hardback Edition 2002
ISBN 1-85937-208-2

British Library Cataloguing in Publication Data

Francis Frith's Picturesque Harbours
Dr. Raymond Solly

Frith Book Company Ltd
Frith's Barn, Teffont,
Salisbury, Wiltshire SP3 5QP
Tel: +44 (0) 1722 716 376
Email: info@francisfrith.co.uk
www.francisfrith.co.uk

Printed and bound in Great Britain

Front Cover: Scarborough, The Pierhead 1890  23471

AS WITH ANY HISTORICAL DATABASE THE FRITH ARCHIVE IS CONSTANTLY BEING CORRECTED AND IMPROVED
AND THE PUBLISHERS WOULD WELCOME INFORMATION ON OMISSIONS OR INACCURACIES

# Contents

# Francis Frith: *Victorian Pioneer*

**FRANCIS FRITH**, Victorian founder of the world-famous photographic archive, was a complex and multi-talented man. A devout Quaker and a highly successful Victorian businessman, he was both philosophic by nature and pioneering in outlook.

By 1855 Francis Frith had already established a wholesale grocery business in Liverpool, and sold it for the astonishing sum of £200,000, which is the equivalent today of over £15,000,000. Now a multi-millionaire, he was able to indulge his passion for travel. As a child he had pored over travel books written by early explorers, and his fancy and imagination had been stirred by family holidays to the sublime mountain regions of Wales and Scotland. 'What a land of spirit-stirring and enriching scenes and places!' he had written. He was to return to these scenes of grandeur in later years to 'recapture the thousands of vivid and tender memories', but with a different purpose. Now in his thirties, and captivated by the new science of photography, Frith set out on a series of pioneering journeys to the Nile regions that occupied him from 1856 until 1860.

## Intrigue and Adventure

He took with him on his travels a specially-designed wicker carriage that acted as both dark-room and sleeping chamber. These far-flung journeys were packed with intrigue and adventure. In his life story, written when he was sixty-three, Frith tells of being held captive by bandits, and of fighting 'an awful midnight battle to the very point of surrender with a deadly pack of hungry, wild dogs'. Sporting flowing Arab costume, Frith arrived at Akaba by camel seventy years before Lawrence, where he encountered 'desert princes and rival sheikhs, blazing with jewel-hilted swords'.

During these extraordinary adventures he was assiduously exploring the desert regions bordering the Nile and patiently recording the antiquities and peoples with his camera. He was the first photographer to venture beyond the sixth cataract. Africa was still the mysterious 'Dark Continent', and Stanley and Livingstone's historic meeting was a decade into the future. The conditions for picture taking confound belief. He laboured for hours in his wicker dark-room in the sweltering heat of the desert, while the volatile chemicals fizzed dangerously in their trays. Often he was forced to work in remote tombs and caves where conditions were cooler. Back in London he exhibited his photographs and was 'rapturously cheered' by members of the Royal Society. His reputation as a

photographer was made overnight. An eminent modern historian has likened their impact on the population of the time to that on our own generation of the first photographs taken on the surface of the moon.

## Venture of a Life-Time

Characteristically, Frith quickly spotted the opportunity to create a new business as a specialist publisher of photographs. He lived in an era of immense and sometimes violent change. For the poor in the early part of Victoria's reign work was a drudge and the hours long, and people had precious little free time to enjoy themselves. Most had no transport other than a cart or gig at their disposal, and had not travelled far beyond the boundaries of their own town or village. However,

by the 1870s, the railways had threaded their way across the country, and Bank Holidays and half-day Saturdays had been made obligatory by Act of Parliament. All of a sudden the ordinary working man and his family were able to enjoy days out and see a little more of the world.

With characteristic business acumen, Francis Frith foresaw that these new tourists would enjoy having souvenirs to commemorate their days out. In 1860 he married Mary Ann Rosling and set out with the intention of photographing every city, town and village in Britain. For the next thirty years he travelled the country by train and by pony and trap, producing fine photographs of seaside resorts and beauty spots that were keenly bought by millions of Victorians. These prints were painstakingly pasted into family albums and pored over during the dark nights of winter, rekindling precious memories of summer excursions.

## The Rise of Frith & Co

Frith's studio was soon supplying retail shops all over the country. To meet the demand he gathered about him a small team of photographers, and published the work of independent artist-photographers of the calibre of Roger Fenton and Francis Bedford. In order to gain some understanding of the scale of Frith's business one only has to look at the catalogue issued by Frith & Co in 1886: it runs to some 670 pages, listing not only many thousands of views of the British Isles but also many photographs of most European countries, and China, Japan, the USA and Canada — note the sample page shown above from the hand-written *Frith & Co* ledgers detailing pictures taken. By 1890 Frith had created the greatest specialist photographic publishing company in the world,

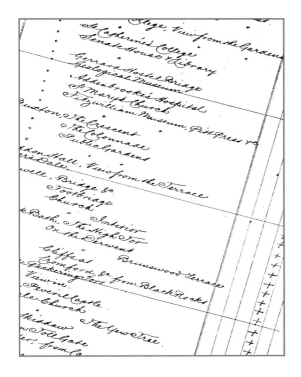

Frith's death, a new card measuring 5.5 x 3.5 inches became the standard format, but it was not until 1902 that the divided back came into being, with address and message on one face and a full-size illustration on the other. *Frith & Co* were in the vanguard of postcard development, and Frith's sons Eustace and Cyril continued their father's monumental task, expanding the number of views offered to the public and recording more and more places in Britain, as the coasts and countryside were opened up to mass travel.

Francis Frith died in 1898 at his villa in Cannes, his great project still growing. The archive he created continued in business for another seventy years. By 1970 it contained over a third of a million pictures of 7,000 cities, towns and villages. The massive photographic record Frith has left to us stands as a living monument to a special and very remarkable man.

with over 2,000 outlets – more than the combined number that Boots and WH Smith have today! The picture on the right shows the *Frith & Co* display board at Ingleton in the Yorkshire Dales. Beautifully constructed with mahogany frame and gilt inserts, it could display up to a dozen local scenes.

### Postcard Bonanza

The ever-popular holiday postcard we know today took many years to develop. In 1870 the Post Office issued the first plain cards, with a pre-printed stamp on one face. In 1894 they allowed other publishers' cards to be sent through the mail with an attached adhesive halfpenny stamp. Demand grew rapidly, and in 1895 a new size of postcard was permitted called the court card, but there was little room for illustration. In 1899, a year after

# Frith's Archive: *A Unique Legacy*

**FRANCIS FRITH'S** legacy to us today is of immense significance and value, for the magnificent archive of evocative photographs he created provides a unique record of change in 7,000 cities, towns and villages throughout Britain over a century and more. Frith and his fellow studio photographers revisited locations many times down the years to update their views, compiling for us an enthralling and colourful pageant of British life and character.

We tend to think of Frith's sepia views of Britain as nostalgic, for most of us use them to conjure up memories of places in our own lives with which we have family associations. It often makes us forget that to Francis Frith they were records of daily life as it was actually being lived in the cities, towns and villages of his day. The Victorian age was one of great and often bewildering change for ordinary people, and though the pictures evoke an impression of slower times, life was as busy and hectic as it is today.

We are fortunate that Frith was a photographer of the people, dedicated to recording the minutiae of everyday life. For it is this sheer wealth of visual data, the painstaking chronicle of changes in dress, transport, street layouts, buildings, housing, engineering and landscape that captivates us so much today. His remarkable images offer us a powerful link with the past and with the lives of our ancestors.

## Today's Technology

Computers have now made it possible for Frith's many thousands of images to be accessed almost instantly. In the Frith archive today, each photograph is carefully 'digitised' then stored on a CD Rom. Frith archivists can locate a single photograph amongst thousands within seconds. Views can be catalogued and sorted under a variety of categories of place and content to the immediate benefit of researchers.

Inexpensive reference prints can be created for them at the touch of a mouse button, and a wide range of books and other printed materials assembled and published for a wider, more general readership - in the next twelve months over a hundred Frith local history titles will be published! The day-to-day workings of the archive are very different from how they were in Francis Frith's time: imagine the herculean task of sorting through eleven tons of glass negatives as Frith had to do to locate a particular sequence of pictures! Yet

See Frith at www.francisfrith.co.uk

the archive still prides itself on maintaining the same high standards of excellence laid down by Francis Frith, including the painstaking cataloguing and indexing of every view.

It is curious to reflect on how the internet now allows researchers in America and elsewhere greater instant access to the archive than Frith himself ever enjoyed. Many thousands of individual views can be called up on screen within seconds on one of the Frith internet sites, enabling people living continents away to revisit the streets of their ancestral home town, or view places in Britain where they have enjoyed holidays. Many overseas researchers welcome the chance to view special theme selections, such as transport, sports, costume and ancient monuments.

We are certain that Francis Frith would have heartily approved of these modern developments in imaging techniques, for he himself was always working at the very limits of Victorian photographic technology.

## The Value of the Archive Today

Because of the benefits brought by the computer, Frith's images are increasingly studied by social historians, by researchers into genealogy and ancestory, by architects, town planners, and by teachers and schoolchildren involved in local history projects.

In addition, the archive offers every one of us an opportunity to examine the places where we and our families have lived and worked down the years. Highly successful in Frith's own era, the archive is now, a century and more on, entering a new phase of popularity.

## The Past in Tune with the Future

Historians consider the Francis Frith Collection to be of prime national importance. It is the only archive of its kind remaining in private ownership and has been valued at a million pounds. However, this figure is now rapidly increasing as digital technology enables more and more people around the world to enjoy its benefits.

Francis Frith's archive is now housed in an historic timber barn in the beautiful village of Teffont in Wiltshire. Its founder would not recognize the archive office as it is today. In place of the many thousands of dusty boxes containing glass plate negatives and an all-pervading odour of photographic chemicals, there are now ranks of computer screens. He would be amazed to watch his images travelling round the world at unimaginable speeds through network and internet lines.

The archive's future is both bright and exciting. Francis Frith, with his unshakeable belief in making photographs available to the greatest number of people, would undoubtedly approve of what is being done today with his lifetime's work. His photographs, depicting our shared past, are now bringing pleasure and enlightenment to millions around the world a century and more after his death.

# Picturesque Harbours
## *An Introduction*

The word 'picturesque' is not easy to define. We all know what it means – that is, until we begin talking about it. Even that bastion of language, The Oxford English Dictionary, states it is merely 'like or having the elements of a picture; fit to be the subject of a striking or effective picture; possessing pleasing and interesting qualities of form and colour ....'. This may be all very well as a starting point, but is neither particularly enlightening nor even reassuring when we try to flesh out and explain what we mean by the word.

One of the reasons for our bafflement is that acceptable, everyday levels of understanding are not geared to cope with specialised, university-level complexities of aesthetics. After all, why should they be? Normally, there is no reason for us to dig deep into such academic subjects. When we are looking at a book of Victorian and Edwardian seascape photographs, however, especially one with a title which includes the word 'picturesque', it would probably prove more enjoyable if we had a deeper understanding of what happens within us as we look.

People's unique differences obviously encompass the whole spectrum of human

characteristics and intelligence. This means that we consider photographs from varying points of view, and here we find our greatest difficulty. After all, what is picturesque to one person could be less so with another, and could even be bluntly denied by a third. To our lay minds, therefore, it becomes virtually impossible to determine any succinct and universal definition of a key word in our book title.

Fortunately, there exist a number of fundamental features assisting our understanding which find generally accepted agreement. For instance, the picturesque is in some way tied up with the familiar, because on opening the book, we turn almost automatically to views of places we know. Also, our interest is linked with beauty - even if definitions of this word are themselves extremely diverse. There is the similarly accepted norm that a photograph, to be picturesque, must involve direct observations of nature, such as panoramic land or seascapes, the depiction of weather effects in water and sky, or the portrayal of birds or animals. The photograph could also include man-made things in an artistically pleasing composition, such as buildings, ports or even towns.

Our dictionary definition reminds us that the appreciation of photographs might involve an analysis of the aesthetics of painting. Indeed, the very concept of the picturesque originated from the ancient Greeks, only to resurface in 18th-century Italian pictures. It was used to describe the landscapes of the Neapolitan artist Salvator Rosa,

although later those French masters Gaspard Poussin and Claude Lorraine contributed their own artistic refinements. To talk of the picturesque was to describe a unique way in which the essence of what an artist saw in nature became stamped with his personal style.

In England, a fascination with the picturesque in art can be traced to the 1740s with the genre and landscape paintings of John Gainsborough, and the developments which followed in the work of John Constable and, of course, J M W Turner. They made genuine efforts to translate the view before them into their own idiosyncratic artistic language, restricted only by the continual variance of nature, their technical limitations and sometimes their artistic integrity. It is from artists like these that we may begin, perhaps, to see relationships emerging between painting and the development of picturesque photography.

I believe that looking at these photographs of harbours leads us to follow a subconscious process. First, perhaps, we experience our first impressions from the title, before we study the entire picture more closely. This process happens before we even glance at any captions. The scene is set in our mind, determining whether or not we find total agreement with what we have been encouraged to see by the title. If we do not need to look more closely at the photograph to identify its content, we become satisfied - and accept it. During the second stage, our thoughts become conditioned by what we feel

about the scene. Our emotions assist us to decide whether we enjoy the photograph, or whether we say 'it doesn't do much for me'. This process of examination is very close to the way we examine a painting.

A photograph may differ quite considerably from a painter's view of the same subject. For an image to be picturesque, it needs high technical and artistic skills from the photographer or painter; the picturesque is designed specifically to tickle our imagination. In a painting we are required to see the picture through the eyes and fancy of our artist. A photograph does much of this work for us by portraying a greater instantaneous sense of the real scene. It still requires us to exercise artistic imagination, but in different ways.

A prime factor of the picturesque is harmony, and this is achieved by creating unity between the contributing parts that make up the whole image. At the same time, there has to be considerable variety in these parts. If the photographer or painter knows his business, a sense of appeasement is created, which becomes combined, automatically and subconsciously, with feelings of awe. Our photographer can achieve this only by making careful decisions about how his pictures are taken. They cannot fall into that colloquial family category of 'snapshots'. Picturesque harmony demands that the photographer must make judgements. It is important for him to decide, for example, what should be included and excluded, or how to position his camera in relation to his subject so as to capture 'that unique angle'. Basic natural phenomena influence his judgements, such as time of day, subtle effects of light and shade, tidal conditions, and even wind direction. These considerations are essential also to the painter, but his final product is conditioned by the considerably longer time he has to spend in reproducing his view and, of course, by his individual interpretation of what he sees. Finally, it is our personal taste which determines the success - or otherwise - of either a painting or a photograph.

The picturesque has to capture an atmosphere of casual tranquillity, of the kind delivered with such succinct accuracy by the poet W H Davies in his poem 'Leisure':

'What is this life if, full of care,
We have no time to stand and stare?'

An element of venerability is also essential to the picturesque: that feeling of being lived-in and lived-with. This sense of age is not merely romantic, and the apparently simple act of looking at harbour photographs taken long ago is not entirely nostalgic. I believe our liking for these old photographs is derived from a subconscious longing to be part of the observed scene, recognising that ships and the sea are fundamental to our heritage. Without ships and the sea we would have been invaded more often, and deprived of much prosperity and trade. Most of us today live in a whirlwind world of e-mails and instant gratification. Gazing at photographs of a

distant past seems to unlock a secret place. Our desire for a calm interlude in life's rush, a longing perhaps for the ploughman's peaceful pace, becomes satisfied. Taking our time enables the scene before us to be savoured. A hundred or so years ago, life was less hectic; the very idea of putting a man into space, or of instantaneous satellite media resources, could not even be conceived.

The imaginative picturesque incorporates negation: there must be an absence of dullness, of monotonous unbroken lines of buildings or trees. The camera must not focus on rows of similar houses, nor on wide expanses of sea empty to the horizon under blank cloudless skies. Monotony is not a picturesque element; with monotony there is nothing to lead the eye, and it allows no potential for more important points of interest.

Harbours are safe havens, facilitating the easy handling of cargoes and passengers in sheltered waters. But they possess also a quality more difficult to define. Most people in these islands have an affinity with maritime matters they 'have a heart for the sea', and often find themselves automatically drawn towards it, even if the desire actually to embark on a ship is the very last thing in their minds. Many people are fascinated by ports and all that goes on in them. Try making a trip to any point offering uninterrupted views of the sea, such as Langdon cliffs overlooking the Dover ferry terminal (see photograph No D50029). Invariably, on clear days whatever the season, a handful of people with binoculars (often safely cocooned in their cars) are always there, enjoyably absorbed in watching not only this famous harbour's hustle and bustle, but also the ships in the adjoining Straits. Ports of any size around our coasts attract their share of interested spectators.

Most of the photographs in this book were taken during the fifty years between 1885 and 1935. Their captions explain their location and selectively demonstrate ways in which the picturesque has been captured. People in the photographs are often an important focus of interest. When they appear, either in those posed views which so delighted the Francis Frith photographers, or when they have been caught unawares, the caption makes an appropriate comment. Sometimes the text will emphasise an apparently insignificant feature: layers of sunlight striking mud flats or shallow water during an ebbing tide, small boats of indeterminate age, a mast seen at an unusual angle, or an item of clothing with peculiar appeal. Our attention is not concentrated entirely on minutiae, for comments often highlight larger features of interest, including specific aspects of major ports, buildings, bridges, boatyards or statues.

The discussion of the ships themselves is especially, but not necessarily, restricted to sailing vessels - a class of boat possessing an attraction totally its own. Although the exact identification of all the craft in the photographs could arguably be

regarded as crucial in a scholarly sense, I do not feel that such close technical detail is an essential remit here. After all, this book is designed more to capture the contribution of ships to the picturesque harbour in which they appear as constituent parts. There is also that perennial problem of identification based purely upon construction and rig. Names on bows or stern are not always clearly identifiable owing to distance, shadow, and even good old-fashioned wear, which causes even an engraved name gradually to fade. Smaller sailing ships like the ketch, for example, have over the years been subject to considerably diverse building variations; these were introduced to equip them better for local trade, weather and tidal conditions. Consequently, such craft had a considerable variety of mast arrangements, sail rigs and hull shapes. Certain regions possessed their own home-grown small boats, such as Manx nobbies, Plymouth hookers, the Lowestoft luggers known as dandies, and Whitby cobles; there were also specialised craft used in oyster fishing. The ubiquitous Thames barge had a considerable number of rig variations, and there was an almost neurotic variety of hull designs on boats used for crabbing, collecting lobster pots, and mackerel or pilchard fishing.

I have included some maritime technical information in the captions to the photographs which show particularly unusual or interesting features; these include sequences of seamanship or cargo operations, and also ports where particular weather conditions have affected their design and construction, sometimes to a considerable degree.

The harbours in this book cover the entire United Kingdom and Ireland. They include both major ports and those minor, insignificant creeks which are completely landlocked when the tide is out. Our journey starts in the south, with the ports of Sussex and Kent. Continuing up the north-east coast of England, we look at harbours in Essex, Norfolk and Suffolk before going on to Grimsby and Humberside, and then we enter Scottish waters. Continuing down the Welsh coastline, we examine some Isle of Man ports before we sail across the Irish Sea to visit harbours in both Northern and Southern Ireland. The large variety of frequently delightful Devon and Cornish ports attract an extended visit, and our voyage ends in Hampshire, at the commercial dock in Portsmouth.

# Sussex and Kent

**Details from:**
**Bosham, The Harbour 1903**  50912
**Margate, The Harbour 1908**  60370
**Sandwich, The Barbican and the Bridge 1894**  34212
**Margate, The Harbour 1906**  54762

◀ **Littlehampton**
**The Harbour 1903** 50218
Although cumbersome to handle, a paddle tug still manages to turn her charge professionally in the centre fairway of the River Arun, whilst a stiff breeze catches smoke from the funnel and ruffles flags. A boy in the boat to the right, engrossed in his task, remains unaware of events happening around him. Harvey's, the Littlehampton shipbuilders, were to survive for just a few more years.

### Bosham
### The Harbour 1903 50912

By a boat jib, our eye is led across Bosham creek, within Chichester harbour, towards the moored boats and the buildings on the far bank. Two boys lean casually, their interest captured by events outside our vision, whilst other lads, seated easily on a small boat below a building on the left-hand middle ground, seem equally oblivious to the photographer.

### Rye
### The River Rother 1901
47445

Fishing smacks ride gently to their moorings at slack water, enhancing the peacefulness of this deserted scene. The letters RX preceding the number on the side of the foreground boat indicate that it is registered by the Board of Trade in the port of Rye, which is situated some two miles up river from the sea.

### Rye
### The Harbour c1955
R77005

Good supplies of local oak supported Rye's thriving boat and barge building industry, and as the patches on the hull of the sloop indicate, facilitated repair work. The boat, with two men relaxing beneath their drying life jackets, represents a local variation from a standard type of craft (see the introduction). Notice the motor bike on the slipway: from the shape of the fuel tank, it could be a BSA Bantam.

**Folkestone, The Harbour, the Boulogne Boat 1906** 53474
A railway-owned paddle steamer gathers speed as she leaves her berth in the outer harbour; the passengers have embarked from two stationary trains. Mobile dockside cranes wait to discharge general cargo (including coal) further along this operational wharf. The crane on a mobile gantry, although restricted to its tracks, allows greater access by reaching more deeply into a ship's holds.

**Folkestone, The Harbour 1912** 65003
The crew in an approaching sail fishing boat, having raised her sails, stand by to clear the jetty, leaving both harbour and fellow craft moored alongside the Stade. We can see the railway bridge linking Folkestone Marine station to the main line on the left-hand side of the photograph. Today, both station and lines await decisions related to the port's future.

▲ **Folkestone The Harbour 1912**
65005
A mixture of schooners, brigantines and spritsail barges lie to warps in the outer harbour. The building dominating the skyline was used partly as a convalescent home around this time, whilst the proliferation of hotels indicate this resort's increasing popularity with tourists.

◄ **Dover**
**The Harbour c1960** D50029
A panoramic view taken from Shakespeare Cliff shows to advantage the sweep of this famous harbour. Langdon Battery (mentioned in the introduction), overlooking the Eastern Arm and Camber, can be seen at the distant left-hand side middle ground. The funnels and superstructure of ferries, berthed along Admiralty and Prince of Wales piers, peek above the sea wall.

**Ramsgate
From West Cliff 1887**
19674A
Functioning still today,
Rank-Hovis' grain
elevator, on the upper
left-hand side, towers
over the hotels
surrounding the inner
harbour and various
craft lying alongside the
jetty. The paddle
steamer may well have
come from London, via
Southend and Margate,
a service which was
gradually developing
into regular summer
trading.

**Ramsgate, The Harbour 1907** 58290
Overlooking the inner harbour, this photograph scans the outer mole and its supporting port buildings. Note the dredger in the foreground: dredgers have always been essential to navigation in this sheltered man-made port, as strong cross-currents cause considerable silting. At the turn of the century, Ramsgate continued to boast a large fishing fleet.

**Broadstairs, The Harbour 1897** 39591
This small harbour shelters visiting boats, as well as having its own share of resident owners. A Thames barge, fitted with a leeboard to assist in sailing such light draught craft, casts shortened shadows across the water. The mobile bathing huts were a necessity - they allowed female bathers that essential privacy common in the Victorian era.

**Margate**
**The Harbour 1906**  54762
This prominent lighthouse at the end of the mole enables mariners
to make a safe approach to the quay from seawards. Its fixed red
light, at a height of 20 metres, helps the entrance to be detected at
night from amongst a myriad of assorted promenade lights.
Inshore fishing craft moor safely in the sandy harbour.

**Margate, The Harbour 1908**  60370

This photograph was taken further along the jetty than No 54762. The lighthouse remains dominant amidst a forest of masts. Fishing boats jostle the large ubiquitous sailing barges lying alongside preparing to land cargo. This was often coal for the nearby gas works. Mobile cranes obviate the need for vessels to manoeuvre into specific positions. Margate continued to handle commercial traffic until the 1960s.

**Sandwich, The Barbican and the Bridge 1894**  34212

This quaint inland port was built originally for Roman galleys to service Richborough in the face of a receding shore line. Thomas a Beckett, Richard I, Edward III and Queen Elizabeth I, in later times, each visited or used Sandwich. In 1759, a Dutch-style bridge was constructed in lieu of the original ferry. This, in 1891, was replaced by the current swing bridge which we see in the photograph. For the next one hundred years, it carried all road transport serving the Isle of Thanet. Toll charges were imposed until the mid 1970s.

# Essex, Suffolk and Norfolk

**Maldon**
**The Hythe 1891**  29077
A long, clinker-built, white-hulled boat lies on the shingle, whilst
other sailing barges and sundry craft surge to river moorings.
Book's Yard at Maldon maintained a strong reputation for the
building and restoration of fishing smacks, whilst popular cargoes,
for larger craft, included the carriage of hay and straw to London.

**Maldon
The Promenade 1909**
62098
A thin veil of mist
shrouds the skyline
buildings, whilst a
fishing ketch, having
travelled the fifteen or
so miles along the River
Blackwater from the
sea, gently eases to
port to take a yacht
safely astern, down her
starboard side. The
wheeled ramp, in the
left-hand foreground,
facilitates the easy
handling of craft and
enables crews to board
vessels in safety.

◀ **Walberswick**
**The River Bank 1892**
29933
The name of this village means 'Walhbert's farm', and dates from at least Saxon times. Two people take a rest on the remains of a long disused jetty, momentarily alone with their thoughts, whilst the full ebb tide exposes barnacle-crusted timbers, and leaves sailing boats lying to fore and aft moorings.

### ◄ Aldeburgh
### Sloughden Quay 1894
33365

A young lad balances precariously inside a small boat, whilst men work on the mast of a vessel moored starboard side to the jetty. The long bowsprit extending across the bows supports a jib sail. The quay experienced considerable sea erosion, and by 1910 only part of the wall remained.

### ▼ Walberswick
### The Beach 1896  38636

The mast of a sailing barge breaks an even horizon, whilst the falling tide exposes mooring chains. These could have become entangled with discarded wire, which was probably broken under strain from a visiting craft. Dunwick Creek, on which Walberswick lies, runs from the River Blythe and virtually dries at full low water.

### ◄ Gorleston
### The Harbour 1903
50423

A brisk south-westerly wind snatches sails and flags, rippling the surface of the sea and causing both the sail- and power-driven craft to pitch and roll easily. When a south-easterly wind blows, across an ebbing tide, extremely dangerous seas can be created, making the harbour entrance difficult to navigate.

▼ **Blakeney, The Quay 1925** 77525

A number of small boats, including a motor cabin cruiser, are left high and dry as the sun reflects on moist mudflats, indicating an ebbing tide. The Blakeney, built two years before this photograph was taken, remains today a traditional, friendly hotel and conference centre, maintaining high standards and offering impressive views across the estuary and salting.

▼ **Blakeney, The River 1925** 77526

The pleasure of children playing contentedly around their sand castle, on the far side of the river, creates a charming picture often repeated with the passing years. On the near bank, adults sit equally at ease, talking amiably to the man standing with relaxed stance alongside the yacht.

▲ **Wells-next-the-Sea The Quay 1929** 81996

The wide, swinging jetty curve leads the eye into the activity of boats and men in both the middle ground and the foreground. A vessel alongside the end of the wharf attracts considerable attention from men on the jetty. Freight in the loaded open railway wagons, at the middle ground, awaits either marine or rail transportation, whilst the distant fixed supported gantry, leading into a towering warehouse, provides quick cargo handling facilities.

◀ **King's Lynn
Southgate 1891** 28760
Lynn (the King's was added by Charles I in recognition of this town's loyalty to the Royalist cause) lies about 1.5 miles inland, where Lynn Cut meets the Great Ouse. A fully ebbed tide allows the rudder construction to be seen on the 29-ton 'Leader', which was built in Yarmouth in 1860. In 1890 she was owned by Joseph Draw in Lynn. The plank serving as a gangway to the vessel from the bank had, until comparatively recent legislation, been the cause of many an accident as crew returned to their various ships after a run ashore.

# Humberside and the North-Eastern Ports

**Grimsby, The Dock 1893** 33272
Grimsby is a major port, lying at the southern entrance of the River Humber. The Fish Dock was built in 1893, when it served the biggest fishing fleet in the world; this fact might seem to be contradicted by this preponderance of merchant vessels berthed in the Royal Dock. The mixture of power-driven ships, barques and other craft indicates the trend at the turn of the century in marine transport from sail to steam.

▼ **Bridlington, The Entrance to the Harbour 1886** 18228

A sailing boat clearing the harbour entrance, using a steering oar to assist direction, has attracted attention from bystanders on both harbour moles. Although sheltered by Flamborough Head, the harbour dries at low water, and the entrance can be particularly difficult during south-easterly winds.

▼ **Bridlington, The Quay 1893** 32050

A conventional rudder and tiller guides these three sailing boats as they navigate into port. Simultaneously, they keep an eye upon the rowing boats, who are making the most of calm conditions to leave the security of this harbour.

▲ **Bridlington
The Harbour 1903** 500

The paddle tug 'Frenchm was built at South Shields 1892 as the 'Coquet'. Owned by T Gray and Company of Hull, this 13 gross registered ton vess lands the gangway after loading a full complemen of passengers, whilst mar others remain on the qua observing intently all that taking place on board. As we saw in the photograp of Littlehampton, these c were quite difficult to manoeuvre; instead of being employed as tugs, they were therefore frequently used on the more lucrative passenger trade between Hull and Bridlington, especially during the summer mont

◀ **Bridlington
The Harbour 1903**
50024
The collection of moored open boats lying inside the jetty, and a few other small craft, make a strong contrast with the crowded waters inside an obviously busy harbour in the previous photographs. Bridlington was renowned for its 45-foot cobles, which were fitted with a small mizzen mast. They carried up to seven tons of coal, and were often used for bunkering large steamships anchored in the outside bay.

**Bridlington
The Harbour 1913**
66246
A bracing north-easterly catches flags and furls the lugsails of three packed boats entering harbour. Although apparently safe, the inner of the three sailing craft could well find herself on a collision course, unless due caution is exercised. The paddle tug 'Frenchman' continues her passenger trade. Seven years after this photograph was taken, she was integrated into the United Towing Company of Hull, later to become the most powerful towing fleet in the United Kingdom. Around 1930, she was employed at Staithes, as a coal hulk, and was eventually scrapped in New Holland as late as 1963.

**Scarborough, The Pierhead 1890** 23471
The disturbed water surrounding the paddle steamer 'Comet' lying off the East Pier at the harbour entrance indicates her gentle movement as she rolls easily to the effects of a north-easterly wind. The wind also calls for an additional effort from the man rowing strenuously towards the quay. The lifeboat hung casually from davits on the port quarter of the ship, and the fragile covered wheelhouse, demonstrate the almost casual approach to seafaring of the 1890s. The 'Comet' was built at Cardiff in 1876.

**Robin Hood's Bay, The Shore 1901** 46795
With a little imagination, it is almost possible to smell the uncovered weed drying in the sun, as a lonely figure tramps with bowed back along the lower part of the slipway towards the boat trolley, just below the sea wall. The cramped grey stone cottages and shops seem in danger of toppling over each other.

**Whitby**
**The Harbour 1885** 18168
St Mary's parish church and the ruins of the famous abbey break
the skyline and tower over the sailing vessel 'Astrea' lying to slack
moorings on a low tide. Built at Whitby in 1826, she was a cargo-
carrying vessel typical of her age. She was eventually scrapped
four years after this shot was taken.

◄ **Staithes**
**The Cliffs c1885** 18213
Disturbed water at the cliff base indicates the power and force of the seas as they surge into the bay and crash against the beach. Calm water contrasts with turbulence as it flows into the creek. Something possibly washed in with the tide has attracted the attention of a man, stooping in concentration on the water's edge.

### ◄ Whitby
**The Harbour Piers 1891** 28854
Prominent lighthouses mark this harbour entrance, whilst an incoming tide ripples the surrounding water, causing the fishing craft ride to surge gently. Clothes are drying sluggishly behind the figures on the right-hand jetty. Just eleven years later the railway came to Whitby, altering trading patterns completely. The piers were also extended, offering greater protection against the prevailing winds that make this another dangerous harbour entrance.

### ▼ Staithes
**The Bridge 1886** 18208
The nets strewn across the railings of the bridge emphasise the importance of this small harbour; in 1887, it boasted over 80 cobles and yawls, employing over 200 fishermen. The boulders and rocks are placed strategically along the mudflats to protect the banks from sea erosion and to safeguard the houses close by.

### ◄ Staithes
**General View 1886** 18209
Upright staves are inserted at the water's edge. These reinforce the efforts we saw in photograph 18208 to diminish the sea's force and to protect the cramped houses and banks. This harbour dries completely at low water. In common with Whitby, it was the establishment of a railway service, in 1883, which affected community lifestyles drastically.

**Staithes**
**Cowbar Nab 1925** 79002
The pronounced wake and blurred sails on an incoming boat show
her quite considerable speed as she enters the bay pushed by a
strong tide and wind. The disturbances caused as the water swashes
around the jetty piles and defences in the fore ground attract the
young woman's attention. By 1925, a couple of the previous Cod
and Lobster inns had been washed away by rough seas.

# Scotland

**Aberdour**
**The Pier 1897**  39146
We can plainly see the fashions of the 1890s as people
meander unconcernedly along the jetty towards the wooden
huts situated on the curve of the quay. A rapidly-moving tide
sets boats awash as they shelter in the lee of the stone wall. This
part of the harbour dries completely at low water.

**Aberdour
The Stone Pier 1900**
45912
A packed steamer is kept firmly alongside the pier as the Master on the bridge plots her progress carefully. She is either about to put warps ashore or has just taken them aboard. The length of the boat is fairly substantial compared to the head of the jetty, so she requires delicate and careful manoeuvring if she is to be handled safely.

**Fraserburgh
Herring Boats c1900**
F63002
The bustling activity of
fishermen preparing a
multitude of boats for
immediate departure
produces a uniquely
picturesque photograph
that contrasts strongly
with many of our more
placid shots. A century
later, this fishing port
continues to thrive in
the face of considerable
European Community
legislation, with boats
arriving and leaving
throughout the twenty-
four hour period.

**Oban, General View 1899** 43206
The steam-powered vessel, positioned centrally in the navigable fairway, breaks the otherwise empty stillness of the placid waters of Oban bay which make it such a safe harbour. The jetty, immediately next to the railway station with its series of waiting train carriages in the terminus, is handy for both passengers and freight use.

**Oban, From the South-West 1901** 47506
With surrounding hills dominating the skyline, and substantial granite buildings, this view becomes immediately identifiable as Scotland. A boat under way gradually builds up speed, whilst a paddle steamer lies off North Pier. The turret of McCraig's tower is clearly visible amongst the trees and surrounding buildings.

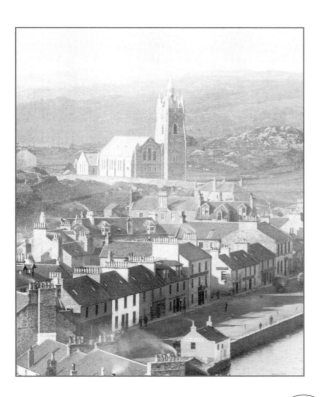

**Tarbert**
**From the South 1890**  T102001
The white parish church, with its imposing tower, reflects a strong mid-afternoon sun to become the feature immediately captured by our eyes. The presence of three loaded hay carts on the distant jetty suggests that they are awaiting a ship. The single mast just visible above the roof of a foreground house could well be that of a Loch Fyne skiff. This was a fast single-masted lugger with a pointed stern, strongly associated with this port.

**Greenock
Custom House Quay
1897** 39814
Dense smoke from a
distant inward-bound
steamer is caught by
strong winds and blown
across the horizon
towards the dockside
shipping in this busy
commercial port. The
same breeze catches
the starboard quarter of
the paddle steamer as
she approaches her
temporary berth
alongside the jetty,
causing her to enter at
an angle slightly more
acute than perhaps
would be usual; she is
allowing the wind to
assist berthing, without
smashing herself
alongside.

◀ **Largs**
**The Pier 1897** 39851
The young man resting his oars in the right-hand boat of the four boats on the left, wisely assesses the movements of the other craft before manoeuvring, taking account of their progress. A man in the foreground boat below the jetty looks with interest at the Frith photographer – this was a time when photography was still a comparative novelty to many people.

### ◄ Rothesay
**From Chapel Hill 1900** 45989
A row of houses, beginning with the headland church tower, lies almost subdued below the tree-covered hills overlooking this bustling sea port. A backdrop of trees breaks any possible monotony from even roofs. Ample room is available for the three paddle steamers to approach and lie along the stone quay without impeding each others passage. Judging by the funnel colours, the two immediately in the foreground could well be part of the famous P&A Campbell fleet.

### ▼ Irvine
**The Harbour 1904** 53154
A rapidly shelving beach on the left-hand side contrasts strongly with the gently sloping mud flats on the other side of this river. Caught in the mist, a row of masts on some fairly large sailing ships offers an indication of how important this port was to the turn of the century shipping and trade.

### ◄ Newhaven
**The Harbour from Hawthornden 1897**
39138
Founded in 1488 by King James III, this port was for many years a strong centre of Scottish ship building; also, up until the time of our photograph, it experienced a phenomenally lucrative boom in herring fishing. The unnaturally stiff stance of the boys at the jetty end indicates that they probably posed for this shot.

◄ **Castletown
Castle Rushen c1885**
C477501
This port lies at the southern tip of the Isle of Man. The registration CT indicates that the boat is assigned to this port. CN, which might perhaps have been considered appropriate, was assigned to Campbeltown in Kilbrannan Sound, Scotland.

# The Isle of Man Wales and Northern Ireland

◄ **Ramsey**
**The Harbour 1893** 33062
Numerous buildings, including the church, the Royal Oak dining rooms, the Union Hotel and the Alexandra Hotel, indicate the importance of Ramsey harbour as the second largest in the Isle of Man. Sunlight, calm low water, boats, and a temporarily discarded mooring rope hanging from a stone jetty, exemplify that kind of minutiae which contribute towards the ideal picturesque photograph.

◄ **Port St Mary**
**The Harbour**
**1893** 33035
Lying opposite Castletown in Carrickey Bay, the inner harbour dries completely at low water, exposing an varied array of assorted weed and barnacle-covered rocks. Two people in the white boat lower sails as they bring their craft alongside the jetty.

▼ **Peel, The Castle 1893** 33048

The castle ruins lie on the River Neb; the castle once protected this port entrance on the west side of the island. The man standing in the boat crowded with people shoves it off from the jetty steps, whilst a seated colleague lowers an oar in preparation for getting under way.

▼ **Conway, The Estuary 1930** 83721

Moored pleasure boats swing easily to a strong tide as weak sunlight dapples rippled waves along the river bay. Trees, sailing yachts and the foreground stone wall contrast with the darker hills overlooking Llandudno in the distance.

▲ **Conway**
**The River 1930** 83722

The two men pose in the wooden flush-built boat, 'White Heather'. In the middle ground, in front of the church nestling below the humped hills, carriages in the siding await an engine. The railway here lies potentially dangerously close to the water's edge

◀ **Caernarvon**
**The Boats 1890** 23108
Sails are being raised on the clinker-built boat as she prepares to get under way and enter the Menai Strait. The sails contrast strongly with the forest of masts from the background boats and the sturdy dominance of this very famous Welsh castle. The calm, barely rippled water reflects diffused rays from an equally liquid sun.

### ▼ Portmadoc, The Harbour 1894  34684

In the middle ground, a substantial stone bridge supports the road connecting Greaves Wharf with South Snowden jetty. This man-made harbour was built originally for exporting slate. The trade reached its peak in 1873, some years before this photograph was taken.

### ▼ Portmadoc, The Harbour 1908  60719

A mixture of craft lie alongside the jetty awaiting to load. Perhaps a rather surprising feature, in view of the date, is the battery of telephone wires on the telegraph pole at the road entrance to the yard.

### ▲ Barmouth
### The Quay 1889  21707

In keeping with the traffic many ports, the coming of the railway here in 1867 sounded the death knell commercial shipping. A strong tidal stream runs in this harbour, and the clearance beneath the railway bridge is about five metres, thus considerably restricting the navigation the River Mawddach for larger vessels. The desert horse drawn carts, and the mirror-calm water, make their own contribution towards the stillness of the peaceful scene.

◀ **Barmouth
The Harbour 1913** 65887
Hanging the sails out to dry
along the railings are as
equal a part of small vessel
maintenance as working on
the hull  note the man by
the upturned boat on the
left-hand side. He is
doubtless receiving helpful
advice in discussion with
the men leaning on the
rails, his fellow fishermen.

### ▼ Aberdovey, The Harbour 1901  46976

The ornamental cannons, mounted on far too new-looking carriages, add a romantic if not very realistic contribution to this scene. More practical are the Welsh coastal schooners, which are lying alongside the moles comprising the jetties of the harbour, possibly awaiting copper or lead cargoes mined locally. The main stem of the jetty continues to serve craft belonging to the Outward Bound Sea School.

### ▼ Tenby, The Harbour 1890  28041

Children playing on boats and beach evoke a scene typical of the fascination of British people with maritime matters from an early age. Sailing trawlers were part of a major fleet in this port until 1888, when the Great Western railway opened its large fish dock in nearby Milford Haven.

### ▲ Tenby The Harbour 1925

77263

Castle Hill is virtually hidden by residential buildings, at the top right-hand side, whilst St Catherine's statue on the hillock dominates the sky line. The Royal Victoria pier was opened in 1899; it enabled Tenby to be included in what was then a newly-created passenger service along the coast. An open two-masted lugger lies port side to the jetty.

◄ **Bangor**
**Longhole 1897** 40248
Longhole is the name given to a curiously-shaped channel, bordered by the north-easterly arm of the North Breakwater, which leads inland towards the central pier. The man standing on the jetty, in the right-hand middle ground inland of the lamp-post, gesticulates with his left arm as he addresses the small group seated in front of him; they appear to be listening attentively.

**Bangor, General View 1897** 40235
The movement of the people along the road in the fore ground contrasts with a swimmer just off the rocks, the extended breakwater and a static paddle steamer lying at the end of the jetty. A paddle steamer plies for trade at the pier end; it contrasts with the rapt inaction of a group of four small boys, who balance precariously on a wooden structure, near the end of the stone building.

**Carrickfergus, The Harbour c1897** 40281
A safely loaded rowing boat is pushed away from the stone quay of the commercial harbour leading out into Belfast Lough. It is interesting that the boatman is using an oar on the starboard side, and is watching the effect on the craft as the boy standing with both hands on the port oar takes the strain on the rowlock. Clearly, he does not want the boy to exert too much pressure and so counteract his own actions, which would turn the boat too quickly and make it collide with the moored craft ahead. Together, they can control the boat until it is in open water, where it will be safer and easier to turn.

**Howth**
**The Harbour 1897**  39297
The streamlined hull of this Dublin-registered fishing vessel is seen
to advantage as the tide laps gently around the stern. The fenders,
which prevent chafing and damage to woodwork as the craft closes
with jetties and other boats, differ little to those still in use for the
same purpose over a century later.

◀ **Watchet**
**The Harbour 1927** 80596
The horse-drawn carts in the fore ground have yet to be superseded by motor transport, even in this comparatively late stage of mechanised development. The timber and bales have either been recently landed and are awaiting the services of the carts, or have just been off-loaded to await shipment. The new jetty was constructed in 1907; it was designed to take motor ships of around 500 gross registered tons.

# Somerset, Devon and Cornwall

◄ **Watchet**
**The Harbour 1904** 52860
The sleek lines of the yacht and the paddle steamer lying easily by the quay provide delicate contrast to the outward-bound passenger vessel as she gradually increases speed to obtain steerage way. Once outside the speed limit restrictions (usually about six knots) imposed by the harbour master to prevent damage to the piles of jetties and quays, she will increase to full ahead, which for a power-driven craft of this class would be around ten knots.

◄ **Minehead**
**The Harbour 1888** 20888
Nestling below the tree and shrub covered cliffs, with (on this occasion) sun-drenched water, this popular seaside resort has always attracted not only regular tourists but, appropriately, a Sailors' Home for retired mariners. The original quay was built in 1616. Over the years it was fitted with vertical and horizontal posts to protect the jetty from natural wave erosion, and both quay and ships against possible rubbing damage.

**Minehead, The Quay 1897** 40331
This photograph was taken from a position similar to No 20888. The scene has changed little in the nine
intervening years. The mobile crane indicates that the jetty continues to work cargo with visiting coastal schooners,
which is doubtless stowed in the adjoining warehouse.

**Minehead**
**The Harbour 1927** 80618
This photograph was taken close to the slipway we saw in the other shots.
The seaward view indicates the protection offered to shipping from rough
seas, and the sheltered beach. There are seven warps keeping the three-
masted schooner alongside the quay; the same number of lines, in a similar
disposition, would be used by large ocean-going cargo ships in the same
circumstances. The craft moored just off her port side is a sailing ketch.

### ▼ Porlock Weir, The Harbour 1907 58365

This small harbour lacks navigation lights and is used by day only. The substantial stone jetty is made from locally-quarried rock. The different styles and materials used in the construction of the surrounding buildings indicates how the little port developed.

### ▼ Porlock Weir, The Shore 1929 82180

The man handling the tiller of the furthest boat moves swiftly away from the nearer craft. The trend of the wake could indicate that he has just brought out from shore the man standing in the stern of his foreground boat.

### ▲ Porlock Weir The Quay 1929 82188

The name of the small boat, 'Emily', and that of her owner, one T Ley of Porlock Weir, can be readily identified from the stern sheets. The sail, to assist in steering as much as in propulsion, is hanging loosely from the aft mast so that it can dry in the wind. The dock used to take fairly large vessels, but major cargoes have not been worked here since the 1950s.

### ◄ Ilfracombe
### From Hillsborough 1894
33433

The carefully-planned construction of this delightful harbour is revealed here. A typical stone quay protects the inner mole to provide safe anchorage for a variety of small craft; for a number of years previously, it had allowed the berthing of large ocean-going ships and coastal traders. The pier, which was completed in 1873, has two paddle steamers moored alongside - they are too distant for accurate identification.

**Ilfracombe
From Hillsborough
1906** 56783A
Still in use twelve years
after photograph No
33433, three paddle
steamers (the two
closest possibly owned
by P&A Campbell)
indicate the continuing
popularity of this port's
passenger excursion
traffic, especially to
Bristol and South
Wales. The outer ship
has moved forward,
allowing the larger,
previously centre
steamer to go astern
and leave her berth in
safety with a full
complement of people.

◄ **Clovelly**
**The Harbour 1890**
24770
The wind-rippled water sets the craft pitching and rolling gently as the man in the nearest lower foreground boat attends to its moorings, with one eye anticipating its motion. Small boats were used effectively in this harbour to ferry passengers to and from the paddle steamers anchored off-shore.

### Appledore
**The Quay 1923** 75145

The full tide brings its own burst of activity, as small passenger boats in an orderly seamanlike manner position themselves to approach the slipway. Wicker baskets carried by the ladies (in the right-hand rowing boat) were very much a feature of life until quite recent times. This boat is awaiting its turn to come alongside, once the other two have been sculled a safe distance from the water-soaked landing place. Ladies at this time continued to be handicapped by long swishing skirts.

### Boscastle
**The Harbour 1893**

33606

The loosely-coiled mooring ropes, the lobster pots, the Admiralty-style boat anchor and the nets provide clear evidence of a thriving fishing port, although the jetty was used also at this time for the landing of coal cargoes.

### Boscastle
**The Harbour 1894**

33604

The natural setting of this small port between cliff faces is idyllic. This picture shows how effectively it provides safe shelter for the limited number of craft it can hold. The one-time watch tower on the hillside overlooks the surrounding waters. A clutter of boat equipment and fishing gear lie in casually haphazard fashion at the end of the stone jetty.

▼ **Padstow, The Harbour 1888** 21213
This view of sailing barges stern to emphasises the ratio in length and beam possessed by these squat yet solid craft. As sea boats, they would ride the waves with a distinctive rolling motion in anything other than light airs with low swell.

▼ **Padstow, The Harbour 1901** 47714
The waxed straw hat of the man stooping in attendance on his open rowing boat provided waterproof protection against the elements. Different shapes and sizes of craft indicate the variety of classes catered for by this versatile harbour, which at one time was an active centre for ship building and repair.

▲ **Padstow
The Quay 1910** 69710
The attention of the children and the men is attracted momentarily from the movements of ships and the sea by the novelty of a camera. The shyness of the girl running to rejoin her group is virtually tangible, but the studied casualness of all involved indicate that the subjects posed for this view, rather than being caught naturally about their business. A large power-driven coaster lies at the jetty served by the corn store, and the letters PW on the port bow of the moored craft are the registration letters assigned to fishing boats in this port.

◀ **Newquay
The Harbour
1907** 59326
The gently
lapping waves,
resulting from
low swell,
indicate clearly
how solid granite
walls deflect the
force of even a
slight sea. The
white circular
construction next
to the shelter
helps mariners
find the harbour
entrance quickly
during the hours
of daylight.

▼ **Newquay, The Harbour 1907** 59328

The numerous fishing and work boats, which lie in an orderly way upon the mudflats awaiting the next high water, belie the fact that just a few years earlier, Newquay was a major port involved in handling a variety of cargoes for both import and export, including coal and tin respectively.

▼ **Porth, The Harbour 1887** 20283

Shingle and mud provide excellent holding ground for the anchor of this solitary schooner, which is also made fast with an after mooring. The draft marks indicate not only how much water she draws once loaded, but also, by comparing the marks on each side, whether or not she is sitting on an even keel. It remains a load line stipulation that draft marks on larger ships are also etched onto the stern.

▲ **St Ives**
**The Harbour 1892** 31158

The boys in the boat demonstrate that youngsters and the sea can rarely be separated. Whilst one sculls from the stern, the youngster in the bows keeps a keen look out. The man steers his craft to pass astern of the boys' boat, whilst the fishing boats provide an impressive backdrop. This harbour was once the home port of the thriving Hain Steamship Company, now, alas (and similar to many other major shipping companies), no more.

◀ **Scilly Isles**
**St Mary's, The Harbour c1899**
S73312
The boat lying on the beach in the fore ground, in Hugh Town harbour, is vaguely reminiscent of an ex-ships' lifeboat, and shows the rugged clinker-built construction of this type of craft. The ropes fixed at intervals along the gunwale would help anyone in the water cling onto the craft until they could be assisted in board.

**Mousehole**
**General View 1927** 79945
Renowned for centuries as a fishing village, 'Mowzell' affords excellent
protection from south-westerly winds. By the time this photograph was
taken, the emphasis had shifted towards the leisure industry, which is
evident from the  small fleet of anchored cabin cruisers.

**Mousehole, The Harbour 1927** 79949
A closer view of this charming harbour shows the perennial interest of local residents and tourists alike in the pleasures that can be got from working small boats. The small child paddling beside the foreground craft is the only one in the various posed groups who is unconcerned by the photographer's interest.

**Newlyn, The Harbour 1895** 36169

A forest of masts indicate the proximity one to another of the boats in the inner harbour. The letters PZ and the numbers on the port bows of the right-hand craft indicate registration in the nearby port of Penzance. Newlyn was considered too small as a port to be ascribed its own registration letters.

**Newlyn, Landing Fish 1906** 56521

Putting ashore the catch is a perennial attraction for bystanders on any jetty. These, judging by the smartness of their dress (complete with pocket handkerchief), are clearly not fishermen. The lantern in the after part of the fishing boat was by this time a legal requirement, as well, of course, as providing light for the men to work by during night hours. The letters SS denote a boat registered in the port of St Ives. The midships wheel, lying fore and aft, was used to make easier the back-breaking task of hoisting sails.

**Newlyn**
**Fishermen 1906** 56532
For many boys, as they became teenagers, following their fathers
and brothers into the fishing industry was an acceptable (and often
the only) way of life at a time when opportunities for extended
education were rare. Note the variety of headgear, and the donkey-
drawn runabout with its large solid wheels.

▼ **Newlyn, The Harbour 1908** 61241

The sign against the side of the shop, above the window and entrance, reads 'R.E. Seigh - Grocer and Provision Dealer. Shipping Supplied'. Large signs were a common method, at the turn of the last century, to advertise wares and services. Children on the steep road and the slipway add a different and interesting focus to the picture.

▼ **Newlyn, The Harbour 1913** 66007

A flotilla of assorted sailing vessels speed on the ebb tide towards the light house marking the harbour entrance, whilst a lone sculler (to the lower left) makes ponderous progress as he battles with adverse currents. Although the harbour is accessible in all states of the tide, south-easterly winds cause a heavy swell to enter the harbour, necessitating caution when navigating the entrance.

▲ **Penzance
The Harbour 1890**
22974

The dry dock served by boat builders and repairers has half solid swing gates maintaining the level of the water. On the jetty, the capstan, with holes for manually-operated turning bars, would assist ships entering dock by helping warp them round the knuckle to the entrance.

◀ **Penzance**
**The Harbour and St Michael's Mount 1908** 60982
The four men looking over the side the boat in the foreground are concentrating totally on possibly adjusting fenders or lines between their boat and another sandwiched alongside the jetty. Ships using the quayside here provided their own protective gear, which was often made from bundles of old mooring ropes. Although the bollards indicate safe mooring, there are few wooden fenders built into the pier.

▼ **Porthleven, The Harbour 1890** 24513
As with the port of Newlyn, the small harbour at Porthleven uses the
registration letters of Penzance. It was (and remains) a common
practice for two boats to share fixed moorings alongside each other
as an adequate number for enhanced safety and security.

▼ **Porthleven, The Outer Harbour and the Lifeboat House 1908** 59231
The apparently unusually sharp incline of the launching ramp serving the lifeboat
helped a speedy departure from the housing. Perhaps mooring a boat immediately
in the rapid descent path was not very wise - this could cause problems both to the
owner and the lifeboat crew.

▲ **Porthleven
The Outer Harbour
1911** 63641
The attention of the lady
in the fore ground is
riveted by the crew in the
fishing boats as they
adjust their sails in
preparation for leaving
harbour. The other lady,
walking along the back of
the jetty, is oblivious to
everything other than the
book in which she is
engrossed.

◄ **Porthleven**
**The Harbour 1915** 86573
The Commercial Hotel
provides an interesting
backdrop to part of this
port's fishing fleet, lying
easily at their moorings. The
boat on the left-hand side in
front of the man on the jetty
is used as a store for lobster
pots. Little room has been
left on board for the crew to
prepare her for proceeding
under way.

**Mullion
Fishermen 1924** 76638
Fishermen with their nets and
lobster pots stand behind the
trio of children, who are
apparently reading, and happy
to pose for this photograph.
A medium swell, with Force 3
to 4 winds, whips up a slight
sea to hit against the outer
harbour wall, making an
interesting contrast with the
calm waters inside.

**Cadgwith, From Bathing Rock 1899** 44183
The man and group of boys in front of the centre ground boat are typical of visitors to any sea shore, and form the kind of scene that has not changed over the years. Their attention has been attracted by a fisherman handling a box on the beach, which could have been handed down by the person inside the boat.

**Cadgwith, The Cove 1931** 84285
The rugged nature of the cliffs is typical of the Cornish coastline, where at low water level jagged rocks continue to cause hazards to the unwary mariner. The sails in the after parts of the boats drawn well up onto the beach are raised, assisting them to dry.

▼ **Helford, The River 1960** H67022

Lying at the estuary of the River Helford, this small port was important in days gone by, for it supported the tin mining industry. Today, it serves yachtsmen and tourists, but it is also well known for its oysters. Fans of Daphne du Maurier visit this place, too; she based her famous novel 'Frenchman's Creek' on the inlet inland of this village.

▼ **Falmouth, Flushing from Green Bank 1893** 31843

The expanse of harbour we see here is only a small part of this natural seaport. The calm waters are a significant feature of the shelter here, even when storm force winds are blowing outside in the bay. The activities of yachts, fishing and rowing boats provide engrossing fascination to bystanders.

▲ **Falmouth Flushing 1918** 68783

The small boy in the sternsheets of the boat being rowed by the white-bearded man in the peaked cap seems singularly unimpressed by photography, unlike the youth in the stern of the rowboat and the man in the ketch. From the back gardens belonging to many of the terraced houses, individual steps leading to the water front encourage boat ownership.

◄ **St Mawes**
**General View 1930** 83172
Looking directly westwards
from St Mawes, it is
possible to have an
uninterrupted view of
marine traffic approaching
Falmouth, which has been a
centre of commerce for
centuries. A large inward-
bound tanker approaches
the entrance with due
caution: its captain is
doubtless taking due advice
from the Trinity House
licensed pilot, himself an
ex-master mariner with
extensive local knowledge
and experience.

**St Mawes**
**The Quay 1890** 24232
Situated on the east side of the River Fal, at the entrance to the River Percuil, the harbour dries completely at low water. Around the headland stands Henry VIII's castle. This was constructed in the 1540s, and together with Pendennis Castle directly opposite the harbour entrance, provided protection for both Falmouth port and its shipping.

▼ **Mevagissey, The Harbour 1890** 27554
The inner stone jetties of this thriving port provide sheltered moorings for a large fleet of fishing vessels. In calm weather, the rocky sea front of the outer harbour can be used safely to secure boats before embarkation - a source of interest to people seated along the jetty wall.

▼ **Mevagissey, The Harbour 1920** 69794
A horse stands placidly alongside cargo barrels, whilst its carter sorts out the traces. The ketch 'Diligent' was built at Plymouth in 1879, and was fitted later with an auxiliary engine. FY on the side of the fishing vessel, just visible in front of the number, denotes the port of Fowey. Wherever possible, the first and last letters of the port's name are used.

▲ **Mevagissey
The Harbour 1924**
76279
By the turn of the century the pilchard industry, whilst retaining some importance, was beginning to lose the impetus which it had held previously. Fish continued to be dried and cured in outhouses adjoining some shore-side properties here.

◀ **Pentewan**
**The Harbour 1912** 64776
This unusual view of the harbour looks down on the moored boats, and offers insight into their rarely-seen deck gear. Accommodation housing and cargo hatches vie with moorings and furled sails to provide a largely uncluttered area for safe working. A woman and her dog pose unconcernedly outside their cottage.

**St Austell, Charlestown Harbour 1912** 64784
The process involved in loading or unloading ships can be seen clearly here. Cargo is off-loaded from/to horse-driven wagons, along wooden gullies directly into/from the hold of the vessel. Similar handling techniques were used regardless of the nature of the cargo involved, although, as we have seen in some previous photographs, mobile cranes were also used when barrels, bales or boxed cargoes were involved.

**Charlestown, The Harbour c1885**  16771
The solid lock gates leading into the inner harbour allow the water levels to be adjusted during any state of the tide, enabling either repairs to be undertaken or the dock to remain flooded at low water. In this photograph, a flood tide surges against the outer wall of the harbour; it was founded by Charles Rashleigh (a member of a famous Cornish family) in 1791.

**Fowey, The Town Quay 1888**  21250
A police officer stands at the entrance to the Working Men's Institute, established twenty years earlier, whilst bystanders in various groups show a rather contrived interest in the still comparative novelties of photography. The prominent white board indicates Fowey's quay and market toll charges.

◀ **Fowey**
**From the Hall Walk 1901** 47701
The steam tug in the foreground was very handy to manoeuvre, and is an example of working boats which have done sterling service throughout the world. Usually, at this size, they were used in river and dock operations well into the 1960s, by which time the last functional ones were being overtaken by diesel-driven boats. They replaced the cumbersome paddle tugs. The moored steam and sailing vessel, off the tug's port bow, denotes a class of ship rapidly becoming popular at the turn the century, although incidents were recorded of sparks from the funnel setting the sails alight. Inevitably, this led to the demise of dual-powered craft like this.

◀ **Fowey**
**From Polruan 1898**  41966
The two men in the rowing boat on the left-hand side prepare their craft for leaving the quay. The anchor in the sternsheets, and the rope, might possibly indicate their intent of rowing out to one of the larger moored craft, using the boat as a tender. The steam-powered bucket dredger, in the right-hand middle ground, would have been a comparatively recent innovation.

▼ **Polperro**
**The Harbour 1888**  21270
The two significant features in this photograph are the nets drying over the sea wall and the way in which the fishing boat is being handled. The sails are raised, but the vessel needs to be controlled more tightly in order to leave harbour safely. She must not be dashed against the rocks close to her port side, nor against the harbour wall to starboard. Each man takes water pressure on the oars, thus easing the craft gently around the exit. The boat is possibly a Fowey-registered gaffer.

◀ **Polperro, The Harbour 1901**  47792
The conglomeration of boats assembled closely within the harbour are under the supervision of two men, one on the far left, the other on the right. Equally as interesting as the boats are the sheer legs erected on a timber foundation with a runner leading to a hook, and a vertical support on the diagonal, to which is fixed the slewing (or swinging) gear at the mast head top. This apparatus was quite popular in those days, and was used to lift gear on and off the boats in the absence of a mobile crane. Today, it is very rarely seen, and is used largely as an academic exercise for Naval cadets. Also, the Royal Navy gunnery teams used an extension of this gear to run a field gun barrel across a 'chasm' during Royal Tournament competitions - now, alas, no more.

### ▼ Looe, The Harbour 1907  59260

This is another natural harbour. It has an extended reinforced stone jetty at the left-hand entrance. A schooner rides easily within sheltered waters, whilst calm conditions in the outer anchorage enable us to see the wake from a sailing craft.

### ▼ Looe, The Harbour 1912  64624

A tidal race rushing into the harbour is used to good advantage by the sailing boat as she alters course to starboard, preparing to overtake the underwater mooring of an unmanned rowing boat. We can almost imagine the conversation between the man in the craft and those on the jetty.

### ▲ Looe The Harbour 1935
86560

Although this photograph is later than many of the photographs in this Frith selection, it portrays a scene that could just as easily be sixty years before, apart from the dress styles of the people on the middle ground quay. The man in the boat alongside the slipway holds her steady, making it easier for his lady passenger to disembark.

◄ **Newton Ferrers
The River Yealm 1890**
22492
There is a slight current running as a larger sailing vessel, in the middle right-hand side, closes with a smaller rowing boat amidships. Whilst doubtless helping moorings to be taken by the man standing in the smaller craft, this boat could well be used afterwards as a tender to take both ashore.

◄ **Dartmouth
The Regatta 1886** 21650
Although marine regattas
continue to attract
attention today, they are
not as enthusiastically
celebrated as they were in
Victorian times, when they
had considerable
significance. The ships we
see here include
schooners and warships,
most of which are dressed
overall, which indicates a
major event: they could
well have been awaiting a
reviewing officer, or
possibly even royalty.

### ◄ Salcombe
### General View 1935  86945

In earlier days, this port served clippers on a specialised fruit trade. By the mid 1930s, pleasure craft had achieved greater importance. Lines of boats moored in the river have become more streamlined, particularly the nearer of the larger sailing yachts and the cabin cruiser moored off her port bow. The different styles of houses reflect years of developing architecture, from village to holiday resort.

### ▼ Kingswear
### from Dartmouth 1890
25275

This photograph was taken some fifteen years before the opening of the Britannia Royal Naval College. The three-masted warship, with the traditional naval whalers alongside, might possibly have served as a training vessel for potential naval officers. The sweeping bay serves now as the site of the Darthaven Marina.

### ◄ Brixham
### The Harbour 1890
26244

The letters BH on the fishing boat indicate Brixham registry. The ladder, leaning apparently so precariously against the hull, is quite safe – there will be no sudden movement of the vessel, thanks to the taut breast and stern ropes with which the craft is moored. The statue is a memorial to William of Orange, who landed at Brixham in 1688.

▼ **Brixham, The Inner Harbour 1906**  54039
A watery sun glistens on the mudflats, which are gradually being uncovered by an ebbing tide. The man leaning against the hull of his fishing boat can get to the craft comfortably in waders. Brixham fishing smacks were built in a style peculiar to this port.

▼ **Paignton, The Harbour from above 1890**  25906
A number of people, on the beach by the bathing machines in the distant back ground, enjoy the mirror-calm water. The deserted pier with its lifeboat station on the opposite side, and the unmanned boats in the foreground, each make their own contribution towards a scene of undisturbed tranquillity, whilst in the foreground a topmast schooner lies easily alongside the jetty.

▲ **Paignton
The Harbour 1922**
73067
The young teenage boy accompanied probably by his mother, with bathing suit in hand and towel draped nonchalantly over his left shoulder, add a note of gentle charm to this otherwise active boatyard. Jetty and slipway are cluttered with fishing boat impedimenta.

◄ **Torquay**
**From Walden Hill 1888**
21420
The orderly mooring of boats assists any single one to slip her lines and negotiate the harbour entrance without causing disturbance or damage to neighbouring craft. Larger ships are generally brought up alongside the outer quay, both for convenience of embarkation and safety.

◄ **Bovisand**
**The Harbour 1925** 78508
The passengers' sense of
quiet contentment is almost
tangible as this packed
pleasure boat rounds the
harbour wall, and heads for
the disembarkation point,
having cut safely inside the
outward-bound motor boat.
This scene is very much
evocative of days well past, for
today's shipping regulations
would firmly prohibit a vessel
of this size, carrying more
than twelve passengers, to
move even within the confines
of a large harbour with so few
lifebuoys.

### ◀ Torquay
**Beacon Terrace 1888** 21428

The horizontal distribution of the buildings shows how the houses had to be built in terraces, thanks to the town's hilly location. Torquay's harbour is ever-popular as a tourist and marine resort. A pleasure boat prepares to leave the jetty steps, on the right-hand side of the photograph. The larger steamer passenger service, introduced seven years earlier, generally took about fourteen hours to make the trip to Bournemouth.

### ▼ Teignmouth
**General View 1890** 26021

This panoramic view looks across the rapidly-drying mud flat called the Salty in the foreground, and shows the point jutting into the River Teign and the pier at the Den. Numerous craft, lying with their bows towards the entrance, indicate a rapidly-flowing flood tide which has already covered the dangerous outer East Pole sand bar.

### ◀ Lyme Regis
**The Cobb 1906** 54528

The wide sweep of the right-hand sea wall and the outer mole demonstrates the studied construction of a man-made harbour built specifically to offer protection against variable winds and the set and drift of local prevailing currents. The Cobb is part of the isolated North Wall, and was built in the 14th century.

◀ **West Bay**
**The Quay 1913** 65648
Here we have an unusual sight: the stern line leading aft of the brigantine, moored alongside the quay to the far side of the harbour, is stretching across open water, a potential hazard, particularly at night. Normally, the reason for this to occur would be when the ship is leaving port in such restricted water. She would take the strain on the stern rope and be warped off her berth. It is unlikely for this to be happening here, though – there is no mooring attendant on the jetty, and there are no men visible on the ship.

### Lyme Regis
### The Harbour 1912  65039

Lyme was granted its Royal Charter by Edward I in 1284, and it has remained popular as a resort. Whatever the state of the tide or the activity (or lack of it) within any harbour, there is invariably at least one bystander (here, in the left-hand middle ground) leaning over the rails watching the world happening - or failing to happen - around him, with plenty of time 'to stand and stare', as W H Davies' poem says.

### ▼ Portland
### The Harbour 1890
27332

The outer breakwaters at Portland extend over two miles, making it one of the largest man-made harbours in the United Kingdom. The external waters here are notorious: the Portland Race, tidal streams, can attain speeds of up to six knots when flowing six hours before high water.

### ◄ Poole
### The Harbour Offices
### 1904  52815

The delivery boy with his basket, lounging against a pillar of the Harbour Office, seems to have adopted a far more natural pose than that of the lad nearest to him or the stiffly standing men. A sun dial on the wall doubtless took the place of the modern-day clock. James Fisher and Company were the largest owners of schooners in the late Victorian era, and continue today, operating a thriving fleet of coastal tankers.

**Guernsey** ▶
**St Peter Port, The Old
Harbour 1892** 31558
Both the Albion and the
Victoria hotels indicate the
popularity of the Channel
Islands as a holiday
destination across the years.
The brigantine moored
alongside the wharf was a
typical sailing vessel of the
day, and would have been
engaged on conveying
general cargoes between a
range of continental and
English ports.

# The Channel Islands
# The Isle of Wight and Hampshire

◄ **Guernsey**
**St Peter Port, the Harbour c1870** S40007
The sailing vessel moored athwartships alongside
the harbour entrance mole would be only
temporarily berthed, judging by the size of the
brigantines already secured fore and aft. The power-
driven vessel in the outer harbour passes other
large moored craft heading for Castle Breakwater
and the open sea.

**Jersey**
**St Helier Harbour 1893** 31629
The twin screw steamer 'Gazelle' was built at Birkenhead in 1889 and registered in Milford Haven. Owned by the Great Western Railway Company, she was engaged on the Weymouth to Jersey passenger and cargo trade. Notice the travelling crane alongside.

**Jersey, Gorey, the Harbour and the Village 1893** 31677
Gorey is situated on the eastern side of the island, and as the photograph shows, it dries completely at low water.
It is well sheltered, offering excellent protection except in southerly to south-easterly winds. The wide tidal range
offers the man at the stern of the far boat the opportunity to perform essential hull maintenance, thus saving the
expense incurred in taking her to a larger port to use a slipway or dry dock.

**Cowes, The Parade c1871** 5749
This is a very peaceful scene for these waters, with an uncharacteristically dead calm sea at high tide. It was in the
1890s that the Prince of Wales, later Edward VII, popularised Solent racing based at Cowes, although the Royal
Yacht Squadron had been established here since 1815.

**Ryde, The Pier 1908** 60567
The density of shipping in the Solent creates a typically busy scene as a paddle steamer, possibly one of the P&A Campbell line, approaches the pier from the east. This company began an extended service along the south coast in 1897. A large power-driven cargo ship moves easily within the main shipping lanes, outside the packed anchorage on the Cowes side. The spritsail barge in the foreground rides to anchor, perhaps awaiting a cargo being loaded into the boat alongside the quay on the mid-right-hand side. A full head of steam from the train funnel (caught by a strong north-westerly wind) indicates the train's eagerness to be away on its journey, contrasting strongly with the patiently-waiting horse, which is drawing the South Western Railway's express parcels van in the foreground.

**Portsmouth, The Hard 1890** 22751
Carriages standing in front of an imposing line of banks, taverns and offices epitomise bustle, trade and commerce. The timber floating loosely in the dock has been off-loaded from a boat, probably one engaged in the Baltic trades; the wood is being stored in the dock to save quay space whilst awaiting further transportation.

# Index

# Frith Book Co Titles

## www.francisfrith.co.uk

The Frith Book Company publishes over 100 new titles each year. A selection of those currently available are listed below. For latest catalogue please contact Frith Book Co.

Town Books 96 pages, approx 100 photos. County and Themed Books 128 pages, approx 150 photos (unless specified). All titles hardback laminated case and jacket except those indicated pb (paperback)

| | | | | | |
|---|---|---|---|---|---|
| Amersham, Chesham & Rickmansworth (pb) | | | Derby (pb) | 1-85937-367-4 | £9.99 |
| | 1-85937-340-2 | £9.99 | Derbyshire (pb) | 1-85937-196-5 | £9.99 |
| Ancient Monuments & Stone Circles | 1-85937-143-4 | £17.99 | Devon (pb) | 1-85937-297-x | £9.99 |
| Aylesbury (pb) | 1-85937-227-9 | £9.99 | Dorset (pb) | 1-85937-269-4 | £9.99 |
| Bakewell | 1-85937-113-2 | £12.99 | Dorset Churches | 1-85937-172-8 | £17.99 |
| Barnstaple (pb) | 1-85937-300-3 | £9.99 | Dorset Coast (pb) | 1-85937-299-6 | £9.99 |
| Bath (pb) | 1-85937419-0 | £9.99 | Dorset Living Memories | 1-85937-210-4 | £14.99 |
| Bedford (pb) | 1-85937-205-8 | £9.99 | Down the Severn | 1-85937-118-3 | £14.99 |
| Berkshire (pb) | 1-85937-191-4 | £9.99 | Down the Thames (pb) | 1-85937-278-3 | £9.99 |
| Berkshire Churches | 1-85937-170-1 | £17.99 | Down the Trent | 1-85937-311-9 | £14.99 |
| Blackpool (pb) | 1-85937-382-8 | £9.99 | Dublin (pb) | 1-85937-231-7 | £9.99 |
| Bognor Regis (pb) | 1-85937-431-x | £9.99 | East Anglia (pb) | 1-85937-265-1 | £9.99 |
| Bournemouth | 1-85937-067-5 | £12.99 | East London | 1-85937-080-2 | £14.99 |
| Bradford (pb) | 1-85937-204-x | £9.99 | East Sussex | 1-85937-130-2 | £14.99 |
| Brighton & Hove(pb) | 1-85937-192-2 | £8.99 | Eastbourne | 1-85937-061-6 | £12.99 |
| Bristol (pb) | 1-85937-264-3 | £9.99 | Edinburgh (pb) | 1-85937-193-0 | £8.99 |
| British Life A Century Ago (pb) | 1-85937-213-9 | £9.99 | England in the 1880s | 1-85937-331-3 | £17.99 |
| Buckinghamshire (pb) | 1-85937-200-7 | £9.99 | English Castles (pb) | 1-85937-434-4 | £9.99 |
| Camberley (pb) | 1-85937-222-8 | £9.99 | English Country Houses | 1-85937-161-2 | £17.99 |
| Cambridge (pb) | 1-85937-422-0 | £9.99 | Essex (pb) | 1-85937-270-8 | £9.99 |
| Cambridgeshire (pb) | 1-85937-420-4 | £9.99 | Exeter | 1-85937-126-4 | £12.99 |
| Canals & Waterways (pb) | 1-85937-291-0 | £9.99 | Exmoor | 1-85937-132-9 | £14.99 |
| Canterbury Cathedral (pb) | 1-85937-179-5 | £9.99 | Falmouth | 1-85937-066-7 | £12.99 |
| Cardiff (pb) | 1-85937-093-4 | £9.99 | Folkestone (pb) | 1-85937-124-8 | £9.99 |
| Carmarthenshire | 1-85937-216-3 | £14.99 | Glasgow (pb) | 1-85937-190-6 | £9.99 |
| Chelmsford (pb) | 1-85937-310-0 | £9.99 | Gloucestershire | 1-85937-102-7 | £14.99 |
| Cheltenham (pb) | 1-85937-095-0 | £9.99 | Great Yarmouth (pb) | 1-85937-426-3 | £9.99 |
| Cheshire (pb) | 1-85937-271-6 | £9.99 | Greater Manchester (pb) | 1-85937-266-x | £9.99 |
| Chester | 1-85937-090-x | £12.99 | Guildford (pb) | 1-85937-410-7 | £9.99 |
| Chesterfield | 1-85937-378-x | £9.99 | Hampshire (pb) | 1-85937-279-1 | £9.99 |
| Chichester (pb) | 1-85937-228-7 | £9.99 | Hampshire Churches (pb) | 1-85937-207-4 | £9.99 |
| Colchester (pb) | 1-85937-188-4 | £8.99 | Harrogate | 1-85937-423-9 | £9.99 |
| Cornish Coast | 1-85937-163-9 | £14.99 | Hastings & Bexhill (pb) | 1-85937-131-0 | £9.99 |
| Cornwall (pb) | 1-85937-229-5 | £9.99 | Heart of Lancashire (pb) | 1-85937-197-3 | £9.99 |
| Cornwall Living Memories | 1-85937-248-1 | £14.99 | Helston (pb) | 1-85937-214-7 | £9.99 |
| Cotswolds (pb) | 1-85937-230-9 | £9.99 | Hereford (pb) | 1-85937-175-2 | £9.99 |
| Cotswolds Living Memories | 1-85937-255-4 | £14.99 | Herefordshire | 1-85937-174-4 | £14.99 |
| County Durham | 1-85937-123-x | £14.99 | Hertfordshire (pb) | 1-85937-247-3 | £9.99 |
| Croydon Living Memories | 1-85937-162-0 | £9.99 | Horsham (pb) | 1-85937-432-8 | £9.99 |
| Cumbria | 1-85937-101-9 | £14.99 | Humberside | 1-85937-215-5 | £14.99 |
| Dartmoor | 1-85937-145-0 | £14.99 | Hythe, Romney Marsh & Ashford | 1-85937-256-2 | £9.99 |

# Available from your local bookshop or from the publisher

# Frith Book Co Titles (continued)

| | | | | | |
|---|---|---|---|---|---|
| Ipswich (pb) | 1-85937-424-7 | £9.99 | St Ives (pb) | 1-85937415-8 | £9.99 |
| Ireland (pb) | 1-85937-181-7 | £9.99 | Scotland (pb) | 1-85937-182-5 | £9.99 |
| Isle of Man (pb) | 1-85937-268-6 | £9.99 | Scottish Castles (pb) | 1-85937-323-2 | £9.99 |
| Isles of Scilly | 1-85937-136-1 | £14.99 | Sevenoaks & Tunbridge | 1-85937-057-8 | £12.99 |
| Isle of Wight (pb) | 1-85937-429-8 | £9.99 | Sheffield, South Yorks (pb) | 1-85937-267-8 | £9.99 |
| Isle of Wight Living Memories | 1-85937-304-6 | £14.99 | Shrewsbury (pb) | 1-85937-325-9 | £9.99 |
| Kent (pb) | 1-85937-189-2 | £9.99 | Shropshire (pb) | 1-85937-326-7 | £9.99 |
| Kent Living Memories | 1-85937-125-6 | £14.99 | Somerset | 1-85937-153-1 | £14.99 |
| Lake District (pb) | 1-85937-275-9 | £9.99 | South Devon Coast | 1-85937-107-8 | £14.99 |
| Lancaster, Morecambe & Heysham (pb) | 1-85937-233-3 | £9.99 | South Devon Living Memories | 1-85937-168-x | £14.99 |
| Leeds (pb) | 1-85937-202-3 | £9.99 | South Hams | 1-85937-220-1 | £14.99 |
| Leicester | 1-85937-073-x | £12.99 | Southampton (pb) | 1-85937-427-1 | £9.99 |
| Leicestershire (pb) | 1-85937-185-x | £9.99 | Southport (pb) | 1-85937-425-5 | £9.99 |
| Lincolnshire (pb) | 1-85937-433-6 | £9.99 | Staffordshire | 1-85937-047-0 | £12.99 |
| Liverpool & Merseyside (pb) | 1-85937-234-1 | £9.99 | Stratford upon Avon | 1-85937-098-5 | £12.99 |
| London (pb) | 1-85937-183-3 | £9.99 | Suffolk (pb) | 1-85937-221-x | £9.99 |
| Ludlow (pb) | 1-85937-176-0 | £9.99 | Suffolk Coast | 1-85937-259-7 | £14.99 |
| Luton (pb) | 1-85937-235-x | £9.99 | Surrey (pb) | 1-85937-240-6 | £9.99 |
| Maidstone | 1-85937-056-x | £14.99 | Sussex (pb) | 1-85937-184-1 | £9.99 |
| Manchester (pb) | 1-85937-198-1 | £9.99 | Swansea (pb) | 1-85937-167-1 | £9.99 |
| Middlesex | 1-85937-158-2 | £14.99 | Tees Valley & Cleveland | 1-85937-211-2 | £14.99 |
| New Forest | 1-85937-128-0 | £14.99 | Thanet (pb) | 1-85937-116-7 | £9.99 |
| Newark (pb) | 1-85937-366-6 | £9.99 | Tiverton (pb) | 1-85937-178-7 | £9.99 |
| Newport, Wales (pb) | 1-85937-258-9 | £9.99 | Torbay | 1-85937-063-2 | £12.99 |
| Newquay (pb) | 1-85937-421-2 | £9.99 | Truro | 1-85937-147-7 | £12.99 |
| Norfolk (pb) | 1-85937-195-7 | £9.99 | Victorian and Edwardian Cornwall | 1-85937-252-x | £14.99 |
| Norfolk Living Memories | 1-85937-217-1 | £14.99 | Victorian & Edwardian Devon | 1-85937-253-8 | £14.99 |
| Northamptonshire | 1-85937-150-7 | £14.99 | Victorian & Edwardian Kent | 1-85937-149-3 | £14.99 |
| Northumberland Tyne & Wear (pb) | 1-85937-281-3 | £9.99 | Vic & Ed Maritime Album | 1-85937-144-2 | £17.99 |
| North Devon Coast | 1-85937-146-9 | £14.99 | Victorian and Edwardian Sussex | 1-85937-157-4 | £14.99 |
| North Devon Living Memories | 1-85937-261-9 | £14.99 | Victorian & Edwardian Yorkshire | 1-85937-154-x | £14.99 |
| North London | 1-85937-206-6 | £14.99 | Victorian Seaside | 1-85937-159-0 | £17.99 |
| North Wales (pb) | 1-85937-298-8 | £9.99 | Villages of Devon (pb) | 1-85937-293-7 | £9.99 |
| North Yorkshire (pb) | 1-85937-236-8 | £9.99 | Villages of Kent (pb) | 1-85937-294-5 | £9.99 |
| Norwich (pb) | 1-85937-194-9 | £8.99 | Villages of Sussex (pb) | 1-85937-295-3 | £9.99 |
| Nottingham (pb) | 1-85937-324-0 | £9.99 | Warwickshire (pb) | 1-85937-203-1 | £9.99 |
| Nottinghamshire (pb) | 1-85937-187-6 | £9.99 | Welsh Castles (pb) | 1-85937-322-4 | £9.99 |
| Oxford (pb) | 1-85937-411-5 | £9.99 | West Midlands (pb) | 1-85937-289-9 | £9.99 |
| Oxfordshire (pb) | 1-85937-430-1 | £9.99 | West Sussex | 1-85937-148-5 | £14.99 |
| Peak District (pb) | 1-85937-280-5 | £9.99 | West Yorkshire (pb) | 1-85937-201-5 | £9.99 |
| Penzance | 1-85937-069-1 | £12.99 | Weymouth (pb) | 1-85937-209-0 | £9.99 |
| Peterborough (pb) | 1-85937-219-8 | £9.99 | Wiltshire (pb) | 1-85937-277-5 | £9.99 |
| Piers | 1-85937-237-6 | £17.99 | Wiltshire Churches (pb) | 1-85937-171-x | £9.99 |
| Plymouth | 1-85937-119-1 | £12.99 | Wiltshire Living Memories | 1-85937-245-7 | £14.99 |
| Poole & Sandbanks (pb) | 1-85937-251-1 | £9.99 | Winchester (pb) | 1-85937-428-x | £9.99 |
| Preston (pb) | 1-85937-212-0 | £9.99 | Windmills & Watermills | 1-85937-242-2 | £17.99 |
| Reading (pb) | 1-85937-238-4 | £9.99 | Worcester (pb) | 1-85937-165-5 | £9.99 |
| Romford (pb) | 1-85937-319-4 | £9.99 | Worcestershire | 1-85937-152-3 | £14.99 |
| Salisbury (pb) | 1-85937-239-2 | £9.99 | York (pb) | 1-85937-199-x | £9.99 |
| Scarborough (pb) | 1-85937-379-8 | £9.99 | Yorkshire (pb) | 1-85937-186-8 | £9.99 |
| St Albans (pb) | 1-85937-341-0 | £9.99 | Yorkshire Living Memories | 1-85937-166-3 | £14.99 |

## See Frith books on the internet www.francisfrith.co.uk

# FRITH PRODUCTS & SERVICES

Francis Frith would doubtless be pleased to know that the pioneering publishing venture he started in 1860 still continues today. A hundred and forty years later, The Francis Frith Collection continues in the same innovative tradition and is now one of the foremost publishers of vintage photographs in the world. Some of the current activities include:

## Interior Decoration

Today Frith's photographs can be seen framed and as giant wall murals in thousands of pubs, restaurants, hotels, banks, retail stores and other public buildings throughout the country. In every case they enhance the unique local atmosphere of the places they depict and provide reminders of gentler days in an increasingly busy and frenetic world.

## Product Promotions

Frith products are used by many major companies to promote the sales of their own products or to reinforce their own history and heritage. Frith promotions have been used by Hovis bread, Courage beers, Scots Porage Oats, Colman's mustard, Cadbury's foods, Mellow Birds coffee, Dunhill pipe tobacco, Guinness, and Bulmer's Cider.

## Genealogy and Family History

As the interest in family history and roots grows world-wide, more and more people are turning to Frith's photographs of Great Britain for images of the towns, villages and streets where their ancestors lived; and, of course, photographs of the churches and chapels where their ancestors were christened, married and buried are an essential part of every genealogy tree and family album.

## Frith Products

All Frith photographs are available Framed or just as Mounted Prints and Posters (size 23 x 16 inches). These may be ordered from the address below. From time to time other products - Address Books, Calendars, Table Mats, etc - are available.

## The Internet

Already twenty thousand Frith photographs can be viewed and purchased on the internet through the Frith websites and a myriad of partner sites.

For more detailed information on Frith companies and products, look at these sites:

www.francisfrith.co.uk
www.francisfrith.com
*(for North American visitors)*

---

**See the complete list of Frith Books at:**

*www.francisfrith.co.uk*

This web site is regularly updated with the latest list of publications from the Frith Book Company. If you wish to buy books relating to another part of the country that your local bookshop does not stock, you may purchase on-line.

---

*For further information, trade, or author enquiries please contact us at the address below:*
**The Francis Frith Collection, Frith's Barn, Teffont, Salisbury, Wiltshire, England SP3 5QP.**
Tel: +44 (0)1722 716 376  Fax: +44 (0)1722 716 881   Email: sales@francisfrith.co.uk

# See Frith books on the internet www.francisfrith.co.uk

# TO RECEIVE YOUR FREE MOUNTED PRINT

**Mounted Print**
*Overall size 14 x 11 inches*

*Cut out this Voucher and return it with your remittance for £1.95 to cover postage and handling, to UK addresses. For overseas addresses please include £4.00 post and handling. Choose any photograph included in this book. Your SEPIA print will be A4 in size, and mounted in a cream mount with burgundy rule line, overall size 14 x 11 inches.*

## Order additional Mounted Prints at HALF PRICE (only £7.49 each*)

If there are further pictures you would like to order, possibly as gifts for friends and family, purchase them at half price (no additional postage and handling required).

## Have your Mounted Prints framed*

For an additional £14.95 per print you can have your chosen Mounted Print framed in an elegant polished wood and gilt moulding, overall size 16 x 13 inches (no additional postage and handling required).

---

**\* IMPORTANT!**
**These special prices are only available if ordered using the original voucher on this page (no copies permitted) and at the same time as your free Mounted Print, for delivery to the same address**

---

## Frith Collectors' Guild

*From time to time we publish a magazine of news and stories about Frith photographs and further special offers of Frith products. If you would like 12 months FREE membership, please return this form.*

*Send completed forms to:*
**The Francis Frith Collection, Frith's Barn, Teffont, Salisbury, Wiltshire SP3 5QP**

---

# *Voucher* for **FREE** and Reduced Price Frith Prints

| Picture no. | Page number | Qty | Mounted @ £7.49 | Framed + £14.95 | Total Cost |
|---|---|---|---|---|---|
| | | 1 | **Free of charge*** | £ | £ |
| | | | £7.49 | £ | £ |
| | | | £7.49 | £ | £ |
| | | | £7.49 | £ | £ |
| | | | £7.49 | £ | £ |
| | | | £7.49 | £ | £ |

| | | |
|---|---|---|
| *Please allow 28 days for delivery* | **\* Post & handling** | **£1.95** |
| **Book Title** . . . . . . . . . . . . . . . | **Total Order Cost** | **£** |

***Please do not photocopy this voucher. Only the original is valid, so please cut it out and return it to us.***

I enclose a cheque / postal order for £ . . . . . . . . . .
made payable to 'The Francis Frith Collection'
OR please debit my Mastercard / Visa / Switch / Amex card
*(credit cards please on all overseas orders)*

Number . . . . . . . . . . . . . . . . . . . . . . . .

Issue No(Switch only) . . . . . . .Valid from (Amex/Switch) . . . . . . .

Expires . . . . . . . . . . Signature . . . . . . . . . . . . . . . . . . .

Name Mr/Mrs/Ms . . . . . . . . . . . . . . . . . . . . . . .

Address . . . . . . . . . . . . . . . . . . . . . . . . . . . . . .

. . . . . . . . . . . . . . . . . . . . . . . . . . . . . . . . . . . .

. . . . . . . . . . . . . . . . . . . . . . . . . . . . . . . . . . . .

. . . . . . . . . . . . . . . . . . Postcode . . . . . . . . . . . . .

Daytime Tel No . . . . . . . . . . . . . . . . . . . . .    Valid to 31/12/03

---

# The Francis Frith Collectors' Guild

Please enrol me as a member for 12 months free of charge.

Name Mr/Mrs/Ms . . . . . . . . . . . . . . . . . . . . . . . . . . . .

Address . . . . . . . . . . . . . . . . . . . . . . . . . . . . . . . . . . .

. . . . . . . . . . . . . . . . . . . . . . . . . . . . . . . . . . . . . . . .

. . . . . . . . . . . . . . . . . . . . . . . . . . . . . . . . . . . . . . . .

. . . . . . . . . . . . . . . . . . . . Postcode . . . . . . . . . . . . . .

**Would you like to find out more about Francis Frith?**

We have recently recruited some entertaining speakers who are happy to visit local groups, clubs and societies to give an illustrated talk documenting Frith's travels and photographs. If you are a member of such a group and are interested in hosting a presentation, we would love to hear from you.

Our speakers bring with them a small selection of our local town and county books, together with sample prints. They are happy to take orders. A small proportion of the order value is donated to the group who have hosted the presentation. The talks are therefore an excellent way of fundraising for small groups and societies.

**Can you help us with information about any of the Frith photographs in this book?**

We are gradually compiling an historical record for each of the photographs in the Frith archive. It is always fascinating to find out the names of the people shown in the pictures, as well as insights into the shops, buildings and other features depicted.

If you recognize anyone in the photographs in this book, or if you have information not already included in the author's caption, do let us know. We would love to hear from you, and will try to publish it in future books or articles.

**Our production team**

Frith books are produced by a small dedicated team at offices in the converted Grade II listed 18th-century barn at Teffont near Salisbury, illustrated above. Most have worked with the Frith Collection for many years. All have in common one quality: they have a passion for the Frith Collection. The team is constantly expanding, but currently includes:

Jason Buck, John Buck, Douglas Burns, Heather Crisp, Lucy Elcock, Isobel Hall, Rob Hames, Hazel Heaton, Peter Horne, James Kinnear, Tina Leary, Hannah Marsh, Eliza Sackett, Terence Sackett, Sandra Sanger, Lewis Taylor, Shelley Tolcher, Helen Vimpany, Clive Wathen and Jenny Wathen.

Free Print – see overleaf